The God of Mercy

PSALM 59:17

101 Devotionals in Verse

Francis S. Green

TEACH Services, Inc.
PUBLISHING
www.TEACHServices.com • (800) 367-1844

World rights reserved. This book or any portion thereof may not be copied or reproduced in any form or manner whatever, except as provided by law, without the written permission of the publisher, except by a reviewer who may quote brief passages in a review.

The author assumes full responsibility for the accuracy of all facts and quotations as cited in this book. The opinions expressed in this book are the author's personal views and interpretations, and do not necessarily reflect those of the publisher.

This book is provided with the understanding that the publisher is not engaged in giving spiritual, legal, medical, or other professional advice. If authoritative advice is needed, the reader should seek the counsel of a competent professional.

Copyright © 2019 Francis S. Green
Copyright © 2019 TEACH Services, Inc.
ISBN-13: 978-1-4796-1164-5 (Paperback)
ISBN-13: 978-1-4796-1165-2 (ePub)
Library of Congress Control Number: 2019919955

All Bible references are taken from the King James Version (KJV) of the Bible unless otherwise stated. Public domain.

References labeled (NKJV) are taken from the New King James Version®. Copyright © 1982 by Thomas Nelson. Used by permission. All rights reserved.

Published by

www.TEACHServices.com • (800) 367-1844

Dedication

For dear Denise,
My wife of 43 years and counting!
Who, like my Lord,
Somehow loves me still.

Table of Contents

Only Mercy Saves Us 9
Miracles of Mercy 10
Seen by the Heart 11
His Blood Beneath Our Feet 12
I Shall Not Fear 14
The Auction Block 15
How Can He Know? 17
The Work of God 19
Someone Who Will Listen 21
A Hammer in My Hand 23
When He Was Thirty-Three 25
The Mighty Blood of Jesus 27
He Loves Me Still 28
The Empty Hall 30
Blind from Birth 32
The Man with His Hands on the Wheel 34
Thy Blood upon My Door 37
When Speaking with Your Friend 38
Day of Atonement 40
Another's Blood 42
The Treasure of Most Holy Blood 44
The Source 45
When Death Shall Come 47

My Crown	49
He Is My Promised Land	51
As I Am	52
The Hope of Ephraim	54
Resurrection Song	56
Written in the Dark	57
There Is a Love	59
Frail Salvation	60
Passion	62
The Fire of His Love	63
I Will Not Leave Thee	65
The Gift	67
Beneath the Blood	69
In Praise	70
First Lady of the Blood	72
In Him Alone	74
I Was that Sheep	75
The Cross Was in Gethsemane	77
At the Gate	78
Gladly Spent	80
The Lord Requires	81
Faith	83
Night Watch	84
My God	86
When You Pray	88
Let Wrath Descend on Me	90
Glory	92

He Died for Thee	94
They All Awaited Jesus!	96
His Blood	98
A Lord of Loving Kindness	99
The Burning	101
Heaven Surrendered	103
How Shall We Think to Fear	104
Luck	106
This Man Receiveth Sinners	108
The Fellowship of Blood	109
Do You Know?	110
A Song of Kindness	111
That Which Saves	113
His Father's Eyes	114
Father of Lights	116
O Thou the Word of Power	117
Twilight Prayer	118
All My Days	120
Your Arms	122
My Lord He Hath Forgiven	123
How It Was	125
The Angel Maker	126
Speaking in the Sky	127
There's Hope for All	129
Witness	131
Piercing of the Heart	133
There Is a God	134

He Careth Much for You.	135
Putting Away	136
Father of the King	138
The Stars Would Weep	139
I AM	140
Daybreak	142
Waiting for the Morning	144
All My Springs	145
Into the Water for Me	147
The City Whose Maker is God	149
A Name for Deity	150
The Easy Yoke	152
Your Hands	154
My Rest	155
Thy Son Our Prayer	156
These Three Remain	157
A Rest of the Heart	158
Tears	160
The Living God	162
A Grace That's Called Amazing	163
Lover of My Soul	164
The Rock of Israel	166
Behold the Man	167
The Way Home	168

Only Mercy Saves Us

Only mercy saves us!
Nothing of our own.
Only mercy, come from Him,
Will ever bring us home!

Only His great kindness,
Beyond all mind or thought!
We are the portion of His heart;
The sheep He's ever sought!

Only kindness saves us!
An undeserved love:
Only grace that can't be earned,
Will bring us up above!

Only His sweet caring,
Can ever save the soul!
It's not that we are anything;
But He the Lord we know!

"Unto thee, O my strength, will I sing: for God is my defence,
And the God of my mercy."
Psalm 59:17

Miracles of Mercy

There is a man upon the throne of Heaven:
Who sits with One who never was a man!
His signet, not a ring upon His finger;
But wounds He bears in both His sacred hands!

There's One who speaks on high for fallen humans.
And makes our frail race of royal blood:
Adapted by His ancient Holy Father;
And raised above the stars from earthly mud!

Oh! What a thing, that we be called God's children:
The bright and Morning Star now one with we!
Oh! Higher than the heavens is God's mercy:
Upon mere human flesh, like you and me!

The Highest has given His heart's treasure:
The offspring of Deity for man!
And sent with Him, dear miracles of mercy:
Poured out to us from loving wounded hands!

"… because ye are sons, God hath sent forth the spirit
of his Son into your hearts, crying, Abba, Father."
Galatians 4:6

Seen by the Heart

The miracle comes of awakening faith,
To set you forever apart!

But that moment sublime, that second in time,
Can only be seen by the heart!

Someone has died, in this place where you cried!
And lo! A Christian was born!

In the blink of an eye, there was grace from on high!
Where once, a lost sinner was torn!

Where long was despair, there's proof Heaven cares!
For a new life has just got its start!

And the grace I describe is real and alive!
But can only be seen by the heart!

Though the wise of this world may laugh us to scorn,
When we speak of a sinner reborn,

There's millions redeemed, but this greatest of themes,
Can only be seen by the heart!

"… Except a man be born again, he cannot see the kingdom of God."
John 3:3

His Blood Beneath Our Feet

A black day in Jerusalem!
About noon, so they say.
Behold! Our Lord bears heavy wood,
On our redemption day!

Bright scarlet drops upon the ground,
Have mingled there with sand!
Most holy blood beneath their feet,
Now walked upon by man!

Men jeered the sight of bloodied Christ,
Before a Roman throne;
And did not dream redemption lay,
With this man's blood alone!

Alas! He falls within the street.
Men's only hope lies at their feet!
Another lifts the blood-stained wood,
That He'd still carry if He could!

Upon the tree at Calvary,
A spear has pierced His side.
Water and blood flow mingled down.
The Lord of Life has died!

Now, that was very long ago.
Oh! Bless the blood that millions know!
Our Lord He bore our sins as wood,
To save the souls no other could!

And if that truth we dare deny,
As angels know, such men will die,
Lost, and alone, (though love atoned.)
For trust in blood they have not known!

As those who jeered His sufferings,
On ancient Hebrew streets,
They say, "We will not have this man!"
His blood beneath their feet!

"Of how much sorer punishment, suppose ye, shall he be thought worthy, who hath trodden under foot the Son of God, and hath counted the blood of the covenant, wherewith he was sanctified, an unholy thing, and hath done despite unto the Spirit of grace?"
Hebrews 10:29

I Shall Not Fear

I shall not fear,
Tomorrow's kept in hiding.
One day at dusk
Is all I care to read.

I shall not fear
With love so close abiding,
That gives before I ask,
My urgent need.

I shall not fear,
For I am more than certain,
The Master of this household
Guards His own!

I shall not fear,
For I am in the keeping
Of the strongest arms
That I have ever known!

"What time I am afraid, I will trust in thee."
Psalm 56:3

The Auction Block

He found me on the auction block,
Covered in my sin;
Naked in my terrible guilt
And so ashamed within.

Now, what was left for all to see,
Would soon be sold for naught.
And yet, He bid His own life's blood!
For such coin was I bought!

Covered in my wretched filth,
Like the Prophet's wayward bride;
Now all the love I had betrayed;
No longer could I hide!

He saw me stagger, faint of heart,
For barely could I stand,
And so He took me in His arms,
And bore with gentle hand.

Although still in my stench of mire,
I was a soul of His desire.
Safe carried then to His abode:
With tender words, that did not scold.

He washed me in His fountain clean,
And showed me all that love can mean.
Then dressed me in a robe of white,
That dazzled with its shining light!

I whispered, "Oh I am not fit!"
My words He would not heed.
But smiling said, "I could not turn
From you in all your need!"

"But this!" I cried, "This robe of white!
Is not the life I've led!"
He said, "I know. The robe you wear
Is my pure life instead."

(Inspired by Hosea 3:1–3)

How Can He Know?

How can You know the sorrows of a woman?
You've lived on Earth, but only as a man.
How can You know the burdens of a mother?
Or sufferings we have in every land?

How can You know the world of a blind man?
The world I face in darkness every day!
How can You know my longing for the sunlight?
Or how for two good eyes, so long I've prayed?

How can You know the aged infirmed and failing?
The ancient, fading sojourners of time?
How can You know disease and long affliction?
You, gone at thirty-three and in Your prime?

How can I know the burdens of a woman?
The world of a man born blind from birth?
How can I know the journey of the aging?
Or all the blighting sicknesses of Earth?

I know, because I live within my people!
The sorrows of all human flesh, I know!
I understand because my heart is with you.
You are My own, and all your pain I know!

But bring to Me your hurt, your need, and sorrow.
I bore your sins and now I'll bear your soul!
But press the nail-pierced hand I hold out to you.
My peace I give, and rest you'll surely know!

"… I have surely seen the affliction of my people …
and have heard their cry … for I know their sorrows."
Exodus 3:7

"For in him we live, and move, and have our being …"
Acts 17:28

The Work of God

I sought to do the work of God;
What e'er He'd have me do!
And make a sacrifice of self,
To prove my love was true!

With strength of will, from Heaven lent,
I'd do and dare for God!
And toil give for all my days,
At His appointed job!

Full gladly would I march for Him;
My life and breath be spent!
But Jesus said, "This is God's work.
Believe on Him He sent."

I'd thought to do some mighty task:
Life's mountains I would climb!
Instead, He gave this blessed task:
This blessed work sublime!

He would accept, my arm be used.
For Him I would be sent.
"But this above all else!" said He.
"Believe on Him God sent!"

Believe despite this world you see,
Despite your bent to sin.
Put not your trust in self at all,
But wholly trust in Him!

How may we earn and keep your love?
We foolishly inquire.
"For God so loved, He gave," said Christ,
"You have our love entire!"

"It's well that you would please your God:
To excellence aspire!
But know ye this, all else above;
It's faith that He desires!"

"Jesus answered and said unto them, This is the work of God,
that ye believe on him whom he hath sent."
John 6:29

Someone Who Will Listen

There's many seeking someone who will listen.
And Heaven knows they need someone to care!
So, if you feel alone with none to hear you,
Just talk to Him, because He's always there!

Come! Tell Him of your pain and of your sorrow.
He's up all night and always has the time!
His heart's attuned to every soul despairing,
He listens. And you'll never wait in line!

He understands the heart of every woman.
And knows quite well the feelings of a man.
And if your mind is wandering in confusion,
He'll clear it and He'll give you strength to stand.

He knows the fears of those who love their children.
A parent He, with billions of His own!
He helps the lost and those no longer searching.
He finds His own and leads them back to home.

He is the hope of drinkers and the addict,
The needy and the homeless, they are known.
He's come to call the fallen, not the righteous.
He'll find you if you're helpless and alone.

He understands the aged, the sick, and dying;
And stands beside the bed of those in pain.
And if your sins are crushing hope within you,
He will forgive and cleanse you from your shame.

Do not give up! There is a hand of mercy!
To hold the wounded closely to His breast.
All though you cannot see Him, He is real!
Just ask Him! And He'll be your treasured guest!

"And the Lord said, I have surely seen the affliction of my people …
and have heard their cry … for I know their sorrows."
Exodus 3:7

A Hammer in My Hand

There is a painting of a man
In faded jeans and tee;
A common wretch, a sinful man;
As in my mirror I see!

A man with trembling, failing knees,
Collapsed in arms of Christ!
A man who's learned salvation's cost,
And who has paid the price!

A wicked hammer, spikes as well,
Still held within his hand!
With these and all his sinful life,
He slew the Son of man!

His face shows forth his agony,
To learn what he has done!
And yet, he's held in loving arms,
As he is overcome!

Forgive me Lord and Master,
For all my wretched sin!
I would not set a nail more,
Upon Thy precious skin!

Oh take the hammer from my hand;
These horrid spikes that be!
And grant it Lord, no more that I,
Should nail sin to Thee!

"Who his own self bare our sins in his own body on the tree …"
1 Peter 2:24

When He Was Thirty-Three

A precious light came to our world,
Light pure as light could be!
And shined upon the sons of men:
For years, but thirty-three!

At first, it was a tiny light,
Within a cattle stall;
But grew to fill the ancient world,
And left no dark at all!

But light offends the natural man,
Who much prefers the night.
And with determination then,
They sought to quench the light!

He healed lepers, raised the dead,
And made the blind to see!
Yet, they were set to see Him dead,
And gone at thirty-three!

He fed the famished multitudes,
With bread and truth as well,
And brought down Heaven to our view,
More used to scenes from hell!

With spikes they thought to silence Him:
With whip and thorns and shame!
And nailed up above His head,
"King of the Jews" for name!

They said, "He could not save himself!
Look! Dead at thirty-three!"
And yet, His words now fill the world,
And set at liberty,

Believing souls, throughout the Earth,
And all who would be free!
For none can best that Man who died,
Yet rose at thirty-three!

"I am he that liveth, and was dead; and, behold,
I am alive for evermore …"
Revelation 1:18

The Mighty Blood of Jesus

The mighty blood of Jesus!
So freely did He give,
That all who bathe their hearts, therein,
Forever more shall live!

The mighty blood of Jesus!
From darkness sets us free!
Though it does not appear this day,
Just what our souls shall be!

The mighty blood of Jesus!
It maketh all things new.
And it can turn the darkest heart,
Into a heart that's true!

The mighty blood of Jesus!
Applied, it doth not fail.
Compared with it, all power we know,
Is foolishness and frail!

The mighty blood of Jesus!
Oh! Paint it on thy door!
And blessed all, who put their trust,
In blood forever more!

"… the blood of Jesus Christ his Son cleanseth us from all sin."
1 John 1:7

He Loves Me Still

I sing and praise His holy love,
That makes my heart to thrill!
Forever praise my Savior's name.
My Lord, who loves me still!

I'm not an angel, nor a saint,
Such rank I do not fill.
And yet, my Master cares for me.
My Lord, He loves me still!

Emanuel has come to dwell.
There is no finer friend.
And though I've often failed Him,
He's lifted me again!

My quest, it is to follow Him
And do His holy will.
And though I am no more than dust,
My Lord, He loves me still!

Oh Father, let His holy heart
Replace this heart of mine.
And let Thy glory shine undimmed,
Throughout the years of time!

Then in Thy kingdom, I shall praise
The triumph of His will.
And sing before Thy shinning host
My Lord, He loves me still!

"… I have loved thee with an everlasting love: therefore
with lovingkindness I have drawn thee."
Jeremiah 31:3

The Empty Hall

In dream I came for sentence,
Before the judgment throne,
And stood in fear and trembling there,
But found myself alone.

I cried out in that golden hall,
"Wherefore this empty throne?'
Then said a voice, "Your judge has gone,
For your sins to atone."

"For only holy blood may cleanse,
You of your guilt and shame.
And He has gone for millions more,
To do for them the same!"

I stood before that empty throne,
And felt my dark heart break,
That He, the judge that I'd so feared,
Would die for my poor sake!

I woke from out that empty hall
And fell upon my knees,
And gave myself to Him who cared
And gave Himself for me!

And when I come to judgment true,
I will not stand in dread.
But I will trust myself to Him,
Who gave Himself and bled.

I know my sins have gone before.
I know the blood that's shed!
And I no longer fear my judge,
But love Him now instead!

"Let us therefore come boldly unto the throne of grace, that we may obtain mercy, and find grace to help in time of need."
Hebrews 4:16

Blind from Birth

I didn't know the love of Christ;
Just knew He walked the Earth.
I didn't know how much He cared.
Guess I was blind from birth!

I walked and talked. I ate and slept.
I cried and laughed in foolish mirth.
And had no clue, what He passed through;
For one born blind from birth!

Since Earth began, no man gave sight,
To one as blind as me!
And yet, these eyes He opened wide,
And made those eyes to see!

The love of Christ, it broke my heart!
My soul was won and set apart.
And I, once blind, began to know,
The very One who saved my soul!

What e'er He used, to give me sight
It caused this man to see!
He surely knew, just what to do,
For one born blind, like me!

There was no clay put on my lids;
A deeper cure for me!
For blindness was of mind and soul;
New eyes of heart gave He!

And if you ask, how was this done?
How could such wonders be?
I only know my eyes are clear.
Born blind, but now I see!

"Since the world began was it not heard that any man opened the eyes of one that was born blind."
John 9:32

The Man with His Hands on the Wheel

There's a painting I've seen from my childhood on,
Of a ship in the midst of a storm;
With passengers clinging about on its deck,
Their trusting eyes on the form,
Of a man in a robe, with His hair billowed out,
Who pilots that ship through the night;
Firm hands on the wheel, no fear on His face;
Only courage and power and light!

Somehow, in my folly, that painting offended,
For I thought myself to be strong;
And to show as my work, simply trusting in Jesus,
I felt was distorted and wrong.
I was fashioned for service and service I gave.
My attainments seemed vivid and real.
And I pointed with pride, to all I'd achieved,
With my own firm hands on the wheel.

Then, storms came upon me, too strong for a man,
And swept me away in their gale.
And the waters were hungry to swallow my soul,
Where it seemed only demons could sail.
I clung to the stump of a splintering mast.
I prayed and my prayer was a cry!
And then, on the bridge, the lightning revealed,
A Pilot far stronger than I!

The wind tore about me. The ship rose and fell.
It was all I could do just to kneel!
And tears uncontrolled, rolled down from my eyes,
As I saw Him there at the wheel.
He spoke, and I heard Him in spite of the storm.
His voice was both loving and strong.
And with it conviction came into my heart,
That all of my life I'd been wrong!

From the bridge He assured me, "I've answered your cry,
For hands that can manage the wheel.
Hold fast to the faith that has entered your heart,
And not to the things you can feel.
"I've waited your calling the whole voyage long.
Rest now and we'll soon reach the shore.
Eye hath not envisioned, not even your dreams,
The treasure my love has in store."

My hard heart was melted: His love and my need;
The partnership finally was clear.
He smiled forgiveness and healed my soul,
And never was Jesus so dear!
Receive me O Captain! The vessel is Thine.
My sin and my folly I feel.
Most gladly surrender I, all that I am,
To the Man with his hands on the wheel.

"And he arose, and rebuked the wind, and said unto the sea,
Peace, be still. And the wind ceased, and there was a great calm."
Mark 4:39

Thy Blood upon My Door

Oh! Lamb of Love, I've placed Thy blood
On door post of my heart!
And thus, my life is hid in Thee,
That we should never part!

Remember me, when comes Thy day,
And know me as Thine own!
For all my trust is fixed in Thee,
Whose blood, it hath atoned!

Despair! it comes in dark of night,
But I am hid in Thee!
And there be countless other souls
With door posts such as me!

And when such time, my hope grows dim,
It kindles ever more!
When I behold, in trust of life,
Thy blood upon my door!

"… When he seeth the blood upon the lintel, and on the two side post, the Lord will pass over the door, and will not suffer the destroyer to come in unto your houses …"
Exodus 12:23

"And they overcame him by the blood of the Lamb …"
Revelation 12:11

When Speaking with Your Friend

Prayer is the opening up your heart,
And speaking with your Friend;
Who loved you even in the womb,
Before your years began!

A prayer is speaking honestly,
What's on your heart and mind.
The Ruler of all things, on high,
Is yet a Friend of thine!

No need to search for special words!
He knows you through and through.
You might as well be frank with Him,
He's always known you!

If you have needs to share with Him,
Come! Bring your heart's request;
And even if your heart's not right,
Be honest! It is best!

But do not only speak your thoughts,
But listen for His too!
For though His voice is soft indeed,
His wisdom speaks to you!

While sinking in the water,
Peter cried a desperate prayer!
Elijah fleeing for his life,
Prayed in his deep despair.

A soldier asked in simple faith,
Of our one Master true.
Regardless of your thought and plea,
Know that He cares for you!

You are not speaking to the air!
In prayer there is no shame.
The words that come to Him in faith,
Are never spoke in vain!

"Be careful for nothing; but in everything by prayer and supplication with thanksgiving let your requests be made known unto God."
Philippians 4:6

Day of Atonement

I look at my calendar
And it says to me,
"On this date, the day of
Atonement shall be!"

But this I believe,
Of that day long ago,
Two thousand the years,
Since He died for my soul!

That the day of atonement
Was on Calvary's hill.
His blood was the price,
Redeeming us still!

As for our repentance,
It deepens by day,
For all of the sins
He hath taken away!

One glimpse of His love,
And it pierces the heart,
And the guilt that we feel
Near tears us apart!

Yet, bathed in the blood
Of that once slain Lamb,
He says I'm forgiven!
And I know that I am!

For, once there on Calvary,
Across a great sea,
My Lord kept the day
Of Atonement for me!

"For Christ also hath once suffered for sins, the just for the unjust,
that he might bring us to God …"
1 Peter 3:18

Another's Blood

Each child born from darkness
Deep as night,
Who leaves the womb
And ventures into light,

Is stained in blood
But not the infant's own.
For blood and sweat and tears,
Are yet unknown.

Each child of God is born
The self-same way!
Another's blood has brought them
Into day.

Another's toil and tears,
All given thee,
(And not their own)
Has set the captives free!

How can I boast who passed
From death to life?
The pain was His
And all the crimson strife!

Oh let my claim to glory,
Simply be,
This precious blood,
That love hath laid on me!

"Jesus answered and said unto him, Verily, verily, I say unto thee, Except a man be born again, he cannot see the kingdom of God."
John 3:3

The Treasure of Most Holy Blood

"In him I find no fault at all,"
Said God concerning me!
This He declared, despite my sins!
But how can such things be?

The treasure of most holy blood
Was laid to my account.
And shall I say, the Lord of Life,
Knows not what He's about?

A newborn bathed in after birth,
Will scream his rude arrival.
But in his parents loving eyes,
No beauty this can rival!

For love beholds what blood has bought,
And what a woman's pain hath wrought!

And as this babe, now so am I,
Within my holy Father's eye!
I know the evil I have done!
In tears, I stand, now all undone!

And yet for me a pardon's won.
For through the blood God saw His Son!

"… he hath made us accepted in the beloved."
Ephesians 1:6

The Source

They told me, "Friend, look deep within,
And find your courage there!"
I looked and saw my empty self!
Which deepened my despair!

I found no hero deep within,
For there, my fears did hide!
And so, to find some real help,
I had to look outside!

Ah! Then, I found true strength of heart,
And help for every care!
Just when I took the hand of faith,
And I discovered prayer!

The worldly-wise say, "Look within,
Salvation's found in you!"
I found them wrong! Looked in the mirror,
And knew it wasn't true!

Trust not in flesh! Trust not your own!
Lean not on self or men!
For every pure and goodly gift,
Comes down from one true friend!

Come to the source for every need,
And find His promise true!
"Forsake I not, but deep my love,
Which I give unto you!"

"Put not your trust … in the son of man, in whom there is no help."
Psalm 146:3

When Death Shall Come

When death shall come (come soon or late)
How shall I pass through Heaven's gate?

It cannot be some good that's found,
In dust like me, whose sins abound!

Imagined virtue laid in store,
I cannot trust in anymore!

Salvation's cause can only be,
That love unquenched hath fought for me!

Such stubborn love my dust has sought!
Such precious blood my soul hath bought!

I know my sins should bear me down,
To rot unsung within the ground.

And yet, His love will not relent!
The blood of Christ hath Heaven sent.

And nailed thus unto His cross,
Are all my sins and all my dross!

No coin of word or deed they've done,
Can save the soul of even one!

So shall I trust in this alone,
His faithful love will bear me home!

"For by grace are ye saved through faith, and that not of yourselves:
It is the gift of God: not of works, lest any man should boast."
Ephesians 2:8–9

My Crown

How could I ever wear a crown
Before Thy holy face?
How could I have it on my head,
And let it stay in place?

I know I'd lay it at Your feet!
I know I'd cast it down!
How could I stand before my Lord,
And wear a glory crown?

I'd know just how poor Peter felt;
That pure and holy hands,
Should wash the feet of such as he,
A wretched sinful man!

I'd know who'd won the victory;
How faith had found my heart!
I'd know I'd lived, and yet not I.
But You who took my part!

A diadem of sinner's thorns
I know You wore for me!
Those thorns, but for Your loving grace,
My own true crown would be!

Of course, I'd don Your tender gift;
Before Your lovely face!
But how to keep it on my head;
And let it stay in place!

"… and [they] cast their crowns before the throne, …"
Revelation 4:10

He Is My Promised Land

Within the very house of pain,
In black and endless night,
Here in a place of dark despair,
There shines a holy light!

The Master now, draws nigh to me!
And that is Heaven's door!
For in His presence, even here,
Is joy forever more!

And should I find the glory land,
And He not walk with me,
I'd dwell within the darkest hell,
Of all the hells there be!

My home is found in His embrace.
He holds my heart and hand.
He's all I know of Paradise.
He is my promised land!

No longing now for streets of gold:
Some place on high to win!
For all I seek of Heaven's bliss,
Is just to be with Him!

"If I ascend up into heaven, thou art there: if I make my bed in hell,
behold, thou art there."
Psalm 139:8

As I Am

"Just as I am, without one plea."
That dear old song still speaks to me.

Of holy blood, once given free,
But at a terrible cost to Thee!

Such is our prayer, when first we come,
To offer naught but Thy dear Son.

Though yet in time, we oft forget,
And think to bring some other gift.

Perhaps some good, we think we've done,
Instead of Him, Thy matchless Son!

"Just as we are." And Thou our one salvation.
Our naked souls must ever look to Thee.

Dependent, whatever be our station,
And only our great need doth make our plea!

By faith alone we name the name of Christian,
Yet many trust, at last, their deeds as men.

But even if we live within Thy Spirit
We still are frail souls in need of Friend!

O Lord! let me be small indeed in coming,
And offer no coin of self to Thee!

But only the Son that You have given;
And blood of Him who came and heard my plea.

"But he that glorieth, let him glory in the Lord. For not he that commendeth himself is approved, but whom the Lord commendeth."
2 Corinthians 10:17–18

The Hope of Ephraim

When we grow weary of our hope
For others on the way,
We often say, "Just let him be!
All hope has gone away!"

"Like Ephraim, his day is done.
Joined to his idols he!"
But do read on! Hosea's book,
Has more for us to see!

The Lord, who said, "Just let him be,"
Hath love that far out lasteth we!
"How can I give thee up?" He cries.
For Ephraim, tears in His eyes!

We need to give to mercy's voice,
More hope and yet more room!
At last the love our Savior gave,
Saved Ephraim from his doom!

For, I "will love him freely,"
Almighty doth declare.
His arm it is not shortened!
And we should not despair!

"What hath I now with idols?"
At last! Ephraim was free!
And at its end Hosea's book,
Brings hope for you and me!

And when our Lord says,
"Let him be," perhaps He means,
"Leave room for me!"
For He knows more of love then we!

Do not give up on Ephraim!
Perhaps he's even you!
Do not despair but stand ye back!
And see what Christ can do!

"Ephraim is joined to idols: let him alone."
Hosea 4:17

"How shall I give thee up, Ephraim? How shall I deliver thee, Israel?"
Hosea 11:8

"Ephraim shall say, What have I to do any more with idols?
I have heard him …"
Hosea 14:8

Resurrection Song

Resurrected from dust, when Earth's day is spent,
I'll praise Him who saved me from endless regret.
Raised up I will sing, that He loveth me yet!
Ah! Only my sins did my Savior forget!

His blood it was shed, and He gave it for free!
Praise be! that His grip never loosened on me!
I failed so often! A wretch I would be!
And oft from His presence, in shame I would flee!

To the heavens I'll shout, pure love set me free!
Praise the Master! Not once, did His eye turn from me!
When I wanted to sleep, just lie down and die,
No hope in the world, at that time had I.

He pitied my weakness, and gave of His rest,
And asked me to trust Him! how could I do less?
His pierced hand it lifted, me out of the mire.
For, though I was nothing, still, I was desired!

How could I despair, when He wanted me so?
It was just that great love that delivered my soul!
My glad song in Heaven, forever shall be,
My Lord in His love, never gave up on me!

"Marvel not at this: for the hour is coming, in the which all that are in the graves shall hear his voice …"
John 5:28

Written in the Dark

There's times I fear I would despair,
    I'm weak! I know I would.
Except for this, within my core,
    I know that God is good!

The way is long. The night is sure.
    Give up? I think I would!
But for the truth burned in my soul,
    I know that God is good!

Lay down my hope? Let love depart?
Give up? I know I could.
Except this light, within my night,
I know that God is good!

"… none is good, save one, that is, God."
Luke 18:19

There Is a Love

There is a love that loves so well,
It will pursue to gates of Hell!
There is a love that gives and bleeds,
And all the cost it will not heed!

There is a love that does pursue,
The very soul of even you!
"How can it be?" We ask of He,
"That you could care so much for me?"

The answer comes when we're alone.
"I love you! For you are My own!"
True lover He, who doth pursue.
And even now He seeks for you!

"... Yea, I have loved thee with an everlasting love: therefore
with lovingkindness have I drawn thee."
Jeremiah 31:3

Frail Salvation

They called it just a second chance,
When I was born again.
Salvation was a "fragile gift,"
I heard from many men.

"What Christ hath wrought
Could well be lost!
It all depends on you!"

And thus they cautioned,
"Save Yourself!
By struggle
All life through!"

And yet, He said, "My burden's light."
And in His holy plan,
He said, "They cannot snatch My own,
From Father's mighty hand."

Greater He that dwells within,
Than evil's hold on you!
And He that once began this work,
Will surely see it through!

Great weight was lifted from my mind.
The truth at last I heard;
Delivered fresh, right to my heart,
From God's own holy Word!

"Come unto me and find the rest,
Your heart is yearning for.
Your struggles can't deliver you!
That's what my Cross is for!"

"My Father, which gave them me, is greater than all; and no man is able to pluck them out of my Father's hand."
John 10:29

Passion

The essence of Christianity
Is falling in love with Christ!
The passion of His love for man
Was why He paid our price!

He seeks for souls who can reflect
That passion back to Him.
And when we fall in love with Christ,
Salvation doth begin!

He said to Peter, "Lovest me?"
That is His true heart cry!
The real treasures of our souls,
Are those for whom we'd die!

How find a greater treasure,
Then One who'd die for you?
But Christ already died for us!
And proved His love was true!

He took the burden of our guilt,
And bore it on the tree!
How could I help but give my heart?
He gave His own for me!

"… Simon, son of Jonas, lovest thou me? …"
John 21:17

The Fire of His Love

"The love of God constrainth us!"
So said the faithful Paul!
We are compelled to serve our Lord,
And bring His love to all!

The fire of our passion,
It serves His purpose well!
Just as, when we once loved ourselves,
And served the prince of Hell!

"Woe be!" Paul's heart cried out in him.
"Woe be if I not speak!
And bring to every questing heart,
The Gospel it doth seek!"

Good news, it burns within us;
The fire of His love!
And we must spread it o'er the Earth,
For our dear Lord above!

Good news, it is the light of God:
His love within our souls!
And we must speak it to the world;
That every heart may know!

"For the love of Christ constraineth us ..."
2 Corinthians 5:14
"... woe is unto me, if I preach not the gospel!"
1 Corinthians 9:16

I Will Not Leave Thee

"I will not leave thee,"
Precious words!
"Nor yet, forsake thee,"
Saith the Lord.

Your flesh and blood
May give you up,
Your kinfolk
Turn and flee!

But know that I
Am not as they.
My blood was shed
For thee!

A mother
May forget the child
She fed
Upon her breast.

Unfaithful be!
Yes! turn from thee,
And leave thee as the rest.

But I do not forget my own!
The cross I bore for thee!
That you might dwell in holy realms,
Forever more with Me!

My presence shall not leave thee.
I Am thine own true Lord!
Nor yet, forsake thy blood-bought soul
You have My Holy Word!

"... for he hath said, I will never leave thee, nor forsake thee."
Hebrews 13:5

The Gift

If He wasn't ours forever;
He was just a sovereign loan!
But when Almighty gave His Son,
He truly gave His own!

Our God so loved the world,
He gave more than we know!
His gift, the dear One of His heart;
A truly ancient soul!

He didn't give a triplet,
He didn't give a twin!
But gave the Son, who was His joy,
Before this world of sin!

The love of God cannot be known,
Unless it's understood;
It was His very heart He gave,
In giving all He could!

And this was taught to Abraham;
Who glimpsed what God would do:
Beyond the thought of creature minds,
And yet the thing was true!

His Son, now ever more a man,
Has raised us to the sky!
Accepted we, in the Beloved,
By Him who rules on high!

And to all beings unfallen,
Proclaimed is Heaven's plan,
In this, upon one holy throne;
Jehovah and a Man!

"For the gifts and calling of God are without repentance."
Romans 11:29

Beneath the Blood

Oh, have you come beneath the blood?
The saving blood of Christ?
Oh, are you covered 'neath the blood
That paid redemption's price?

There is a debt we've all incurred;
But written in His holy Word,
A way's been found to make you whole;
For One has died to save your soul!

There is no other place to be,
Where's found salvation's gift for thee!
To save from Heaven's wrath to come,
When sin and sinners are undone!

There is a day of reckoning,
As came with Noah's flood!
Oh, find the shelter cleft for thee,
Beneath His saving blood!

"For this is my blood of the new testament, which is shed for many for the remission of sins."
Matthew 26:28

In Praise

Offspring of the Highest,
The Son of great I Am
The One who made us from the dust,
Back when the world began!

On Earth, You did your Father's will!
And rose above all men.
God gave to us a champion!
A dear eternal Friend!

Who made the very stars we see,
And calls them all by name!
Upon the Cross He proved a love;
Puts every else to shame!

To have the Son of Deity,
To call our cherished brother.
Bestows on every soul on Earth,
A gift beyond all other!

He brings with Him forever-life;
To bless all who believe!
A life to measure with His own,
For all who will receive.

Upon the throne of Heaven,
Beside the great I Am!
There sits in rule, for me and you,
The blessed Son of Man!

Come boldly then ye supplicants!
On high we have a Friend!
Whose love is as His Father's own;
For all the race of men!

"For as the Father hath life in himself; so hath he given
to the Son to have life in himself."
John 5:26

First Lady of the Blood

A lost old Christian lady,
I helped to find her bus,
And took in hand her hefty bags,
As she followed me in trust.

She asked me if I knew the Blood.
(I thought her somewhat touched!)
"Oh you must come beneath the Blood!"
She seemed to care so much!

The church that I grew up in
Of blood would seldom speak
But only by good works and church
To Heaven did it seek!

Now, climbing up into her bus
She said she'd pray for me.
And I remember, years ago,
How earnest then was she!

That's roughly sixty years today!
And still her face I see;
That dear old Christian lady,
Was the first to pray for me!

And hearkening to her fervent prayer,
Good Shepard sought for me!
Now here beneath His saving Blood,
These blessed years I be!

In Heaven's grand reunion,
Wherein I trust to be!
Someday I hope to meet again,
The first who prayed for me!

"... ye were not redeemed with corruptible things ...
But with the precious blood of Christ."
1 Peter 1:18–19

In Him Alone

In Him alone we have our being;
In Him alone we're pure!
Oh Master! Do draw near to us,
And bring Thy goodness here!

In Him alone we may abide,
And cleanse our needful souls!
Oh let Thy holy face appear,
And purity we'll know!

In Him alone we find the truth,
He is our life and breath!
Oh may our souls be hid in Him,
The Rock that God has cleft!

In Him alone, our God is known:
His Father come to see!
"And I am thine, for all of time,
"If you but come to Me!"

"For in him we live, and move, and have our being …"
Acts 17:28

I Was that Sheep

I was lost in a storm of confusion and night,
    And could not discover my way.
Without shelter or strength, to deliver myself,
    All was lost with the fading of day!

I was then at wit's end! So in need of a friend!
    So desperate my heart sought to pray!
'Twas more like the sound of one 'bout to die;
    Like a soul just passing away!

No light was ahead, only darkness instead!
    Yet, my cry was heard o'er the storm.
For One came to find me and carry me home!
    His arms both loving and warm!

A Shepard was He, who sought after me.
And said, I was one of His own!
Though He had ninety-nine, yet me He would find:
The one out wandering alone!

Now darkness was gone with the coming of dawn;
All doubt and confusion did flee!
For the Shepard was strong who bore me along.
And said, "You are precious to Me!"

I was that sheep! And friend, so were you!
Till He who is Love found us out!
When that story is told of the Shepard and sheep,
We know what the story's about!

"… if a man have an hundred sheep, and one of them be gone astray, doth he not live the ninety and nine, and go into the mountains, and seeketh that which is gone astray?"
Matthew 18:12

The Cross Was in Gethsemane

The Cross was in Gethsemane,
For there the Savior lay,
And felt the weight of sin come down,
That drove His breath away.

The Cross was in Gethsemane:
All that our Lord could bear,
He nailed up His human will!
The world unaware.

The Cross was in Gethsemane.
But few would ever know,
From thence came all His great resolve,
Upon the tree to show.

The Cross was in Gethsemane;
Where not a soul could see.
With none to call His battle brave,
Or scorn if He should flee!

The Cross was in Gethsemane;
A secret race was run:
And our salvation, born in Him,
Who said, "Thy will be done!"

"… Abba, Father, all things are possible unto thee; take away this cup from me: nevertheless not what I will, but what thou wilt."
Mark 14:36

At the Gate

There came two men to Heaven, and at its splendid gate,
They answered, each man for himself, the keeper of their fate.
The searcher there of hidden hearts (For whom each seeker yearned,)
Gave test to all their source of trust (And all their hearts had learned.)

"What claim for your redemption, can grant you entrance here?
How do you qualify to walk where holy angels fear?"

The first man said, "My life is clean! Behold me, void of sin!
This did the Christ, within my life, that I might enter in:
All holy, harmless, undefiled! And such a one as He!
All praise to Him who fashioned thus, a miracle like me!"

The candidate who followed next, then stood before his Lord;
To answer Him, whose holy voice, was as a two-edged sword!
"What offering do you present? Do you have Heaven's key?
No flesh shall come with empty hands! Where is your gift to me?"

"I have no gift to make Thee, Lord." the second softly said.
"All good appearing in my life. Christ wrought it in my stead!
He wove the very robe I wear, and made my eyes to see,
That there is not a scrap of good, belonging unto me!

Therefore, my ransom is His blood. In it I rest my fate!
I claim Thy Christ as entrance Lord. For Jesus is my gate."

To whom did Heaven open wide? The answer's plain to see.
No flesh shall be self-justified, nor buy a gift that's free!
All boasted claims of holiness are but the devil's sham.
Bring not to God Cain's offering, but Abel's spotless Lamb!

"For by grace are ye saved through faith: and that not of yourselves:
it is the gift of God: Not of works, lest any man should boast."
Ephesians 2:8–9

Gladly Spent

I will very gladly spend,
And will be spent for you.
Although, I know you love Me not,
And never have been true.

O enemy within your mind,
Behold! I die for thee!
And though you will not hear My voice;
My blood is given free!

Now, Measure out the span of love,
Upon My splintered cross.
And though I die a shameful death
I do not count it loss.

It flows in red; it flows from Me:
My scarlet love is plain to see!
I gladly spend and have been spent,
Since to the cross I freely went!

They pierced my side, I pierce the heart,
Of every harking soul.
Come stand beneath my saving cross,
And watch salvation flow!

"And I will very gladly spend and be spent for you; though the more abundantly I love you, the less I be loved."
2 Corinthians 12:15

The Lord Requires

"What doth the Lord require of thee?"
"Much" saith the hide bound Pharisee!
"Doth keep the ancient feast days?
And phases of the moon?
I bring you such requirements,
Your life has barely room!"

But, what does the Lord require of thee?
Mercy from a tender heart, like He!
Come learn of Me. Do justly,
Love family deep and true!
And live your life in trust of Christ,
Because He died for you!

Come see! His yoke is easy;
His burden feather light!
Come! Learn of Him, and find the rest,
You've longed for all your life!

What you can give, give freely.
That soul you serve is you!
Do always to another then,
As you would have them do.

The sum of law and prophets:
Commandments of the free!
Come live a life of love to Man! "
Do all you do for Me!"

"… what doth the Lord require of thee, but to do justly, and to love mercy, and to walk humbly with thy God?
Micah 6:8

Faith

Faith's the loving evidence
Of things we cannot see.
My bit of faith,
You're living proof,
Of God's great love for me.

Whence came the Earth?
The stars on high?
How did all life begin?
By faith I know God made the worlds
And formed my faith within.

I need no pompous, grand decree,
From prelate, prince or pope.
My very heart declares You are
The substance of my hope!

"Now faith is the substance of things hoped for, the evidence
of things not seen."
Hebrews 11:1

Night Watch

At rest from its passions,
The world at nod,
Makes way for the stillness
And whispers of God.

Kings dream of their edicts,
And all they will say,
But He in the quiet,
Prepareth a day.

In the deep hours of night,
When the World is sleeping,
It seems that the darkness
Has Earth in its keeping.

But the guard never slumbers
That stands at the bed,
Of each whom the Lord
Hath chosen and led.

No less is He present!
Some find, with a thrill,
Their first glimpse of glory,
When the world is still.

His work is unceasing,
Be it darkness or light.
For the God of the sunrise
Is God of the night.

"Yea, the darkness hideth not from thee; but the night shineth as the day: the darkness and the light are both alike to thee."
Psalm 139:12

My God

I'm sickened by the god of hate!
The headlines scream of him of late!
The god who bombs with heart of stone;

He cannot be the God I've known!
My God He does not thirst for death.
He is the Rock for all that's cleft!

A God of loving kindness,
That some have never known:
He of the wondrous saving name,
Ah! He is God alone!

The God of true compassion,
Whose mercy doth astound!
The Lord of understanding heart,
The only God I've found!

Sent not His Son, to us condemn!
Nor doth He sendeth we;
To bruise or wound a trembling soul;
But set the captives free!

The God that hearts are glad to find!
(Who loves us after all!)
The Lord we learned when we were young;
And loved when we were small!

No Master harsh, no reaper grim,
But One who calls us dear to Him.
The God of love is He!

The Shepard searching for His sheep:
The One you bless before you sleep:
Who guards your rest, your soul to keep;
Oh! He is God to me!

"For I know the thoughts that I think toward you, saith the Lord, thoughts of peace, and not of evil, to give you an expected end."
Jeremiah 29:11

When You Pray

"Oh Master teach us how to pray!"
Disciples asked of old.
And we would do quite well indeed,
To heed what they were told!

"When you would pray, say Father,
For such He is to you!
So, call Him by that very name,
As you have heard Me do!"

The One who dwells above the clouds,
Is also kin to thee!
For He hath called you child of His.
And this you'll ever be!

Ye children of the Mighty One,
Sing out His holy praise!
What honor to be called His kin,
The Ancient He of Days!

Let us by faith, before His throne,
Cry Abba! From the heart!
Oh hold us to Thy holy breast,
For Father true Thou art!

Thy will in Heaven (Earth as well!)
Be done! Oh make it true!
Forgive our sins, though we be dust;
We would forgive like You!

Oh keep us from temptations lure;
All evil that there be!
And save us from our sinful selves,
For we are kin to Thee!

The kingdom and the power,
O Holy One Divine;
The glory of all worlds on high,
Forever more art Thine!

"... When ye pray, say, Our Father which art in heaven,
Hallowed be thy name."
Luke 11:2

Let Wrath Descend on Me

The wrath of holy justice,
Lives in our Deity!
Yet, this is so entwined with grace,
That Love would die for thee!

There comes a judgment for our sin;
To strike the guilty down!
But there is mercy with the Lord,
And grace that doth abound!

I know some words, that break the hearts,
Of sinners that we be!
"Oh! Spare these foolish erring sheep!
Let wrath descend on Me!"

"Let Me become for them, their sin,
And they My purity!
To save the children of Thy grace,
Let wrath descend on Me!"

The mystery of most holy love!
So foreign unto we!
How can you say, "Let sinners go!
And place their blame on me"?

It tears the fabric of our souls,
That such a love can be!
Oh! Let the Spirit of Thy Son,
Descend on such as me!

"For he hath made him to be sin for us, who knew no sin; that we might be made the righteousness of God in him."
2 Corinthians 5:21

Glory

The glory of our Father
And glory of our Lord:
The angels and creation sing
Of these with one accord!

Who undergird the universe:
Creation their sweet plan.
And by their word, the very stars
And all things living stand!

The heavens cannot hold their praise!
The very rocks cry out!
And myriad souls, Earth has not seen;
Do raise a joyful shout!

Oh, surely you have heard the love
All things in nature raise;
Unto the Son of Righteousness,
And Father of His praise!

All things of Earth sing out in joy,
But unbelieving men!
Oh that we too, would all give praise
Unto our sovereign friends!

And sing aloud in holy song
In rapture and in praise,
Unto the Lord of all the Earth
And Ancient He of days!

"The heavens declare the glory of God; and the firmament sheweth his handywork.
Day unto day uttereth speech, and night unto night sheweth knowledge.
There is no speech nor language, where their voice is not heard."
Psalm 19:1–3

He Died for Thee

The glory of Jehovah!
He Came! Our Mercy's Son!
He came to save humanity,
But would have died for one!

Before there was a grain of sand;
He knew we'd be undone!
From fallen Eve to such as we;
The sinners we'd become!

For frailty of humanity;
For sin there was a plan!
For They who called us from the dust,
Knew all would be in man!

Before there was an Eden,
The Cross was Heaven's plan!
And If we but, come unto Him;
We'll find the promised land!

He didn't come for faceless hordes,
Or nameless he and she!
But real hearts, He knew by name;
All children yet to be!

He'd die to save, just fallen Eve,
Or Adam, if they'd trust!
For they were precious unto Him.
He loved them just as us!

Don't say, "He came for other flesh,
Of far more worth than me!
But surly know within thy soul,
That Christ hath died for thee!

"According as he hath chosen us in him before
the foundation of the world …"
Ephesians 1:4

They All Awaited Jesus!

We do not lean to Moses now,
Or Father Abraham.
Today our trust is in the Son:
The Son of Great I Am!

For Jesus said, "These very ones,
They testified of Me."
And all of those who came before;
But point the soul to He!

They all awaited Jesus;
Their own faith to renew!
To open Scripture to their hearts,
And maketh all things new!

The words He's spoken to us,
They clear confused of mind!
He spoke as none had spoke before;
His very thoughts divine!

Where once we knew stern Deity,
We have a Father true!
Who loves and sent His very own,
For sinful me and you!

So, now we trust a Brother,
Who calls us to His heart:
The very Lord who died for us;
Who came and took our part!

"… the law was given by Moses, but grace
and truth came by Jesus Christ."
John 1:17

His Blood

To gain the life eternal,
You must receive life twice!
And if you'd live forever more;
Partake the Blood of Christ!

"The life of flesh is in the blood."
The Word would have us see!
And thou shalt gain eternal life;
In blood He shed for thee.

The life begot from Father,
Is His to give to thee!
A life to measure with His own,
He offers to you free!

Your life proceeded from His veins;
Else you would never be!
For every breath that's drawn on Earth,
Is from the veins of He!

And as He gave, in upper room,
That cup, so blessed be!
Remember, and partake the life,
And blood poured out for thee!

"… except ye eat the flesh of the Son of man,
and drink his blood, ye have no life in you."
John 6:53

A Lord of Loving Kindness

A Lord of loving kindness,
The Psalms sing and adore!
And speak of loving kindness,
Full twenty times or more!

Our Lord in tender mercy,
Our spirits would restore!
Good gifts upon all humankind,
His generous heart doth pour!

A Lord of loving kindness,
To those with hearts to see!
Abundant love for thee He hath,
As He hath love for me!

Some cry, "unfeeling Deity!"
Say this our Master be!
But if you breathe upon this Earth,
His care hath come to thee!

A Lord of loving kindness:
If this great truth not be,
How could there come, the light of hope,
To creatures such as we?

The sacrifice of Calvary
Should make it clear to see,
A loving Lord of kindness,
Hath poured His love on thee!

"How excellent is thy lovingkindness, O God! therefore the children of men put their trust under the shadow of thy wings."
Psalm 36:7

The Burning

Across the world
In many lands
Where e'er they know
The cross,

And anywhere
Where darkness is,
And hearts are torn
And tossed

There rises
Like a mighty choir
A longing burning
Like a fire
To touch the loving Face of Him, who is
Our hearts desire.

Now, no such prayer
Is lost to Him
Who is
Our breath
And soul!
And every heart
That reaches out
Our loving Father knows!

And deep within
Believing minds
A certainty
Is stirred,
That none of these
Cry out in vain,
But every voice is heard!

"… I, if I be lifted up from the earth, will draw all men unto me."
John 12:32

Heaven Surrendered

"I would that I be cursed of Christ,
If it would save my kin!"
Said Paul, upon his knees in prayer,
For his lost brethren.

And surly Heaven's homes were built
For others such as he;
Who would give up a mansion there,
To set another free.

For this is what our Savior did;
Gave up His throne on high!
And died the death that we deserved;
That we, His own, not die!

Bright Heaven is a home for those
Who'd give that home away:
To see another won to God,
And live to walk in day!

"For I could wish that myself were accursed
from Christ for my brethren …"
Romans 9:3

How Shall We Think to Fear

If You regard each nameless bird
This world shall ever know;
How close must be Your loving watch,
O'er every ransomed soul.

And since Your pure and mighty host
Are ever gathered near:
Your shining guard about our path,
How shall we think to fear?

If mighty stars are each upheld,
To serve Your mighty plan,
How small a thing it is for You
To keep a trusting man!

What if the dark surround us now?
The light shall yet appear!
How shall we call ourselves redeemed,
And ever think to fear?

We know Your heart has cherished us;
You gave Your precious Son!
Though we are only of the dust,
Our hearts are surely won!

With such as He to hold us close,
Such love to call us dear!
With nailed hands to press our own,
How shall we think to fear?

"For God hath not given us the spirit of fear; but of power,
and of love, and of a sound mind."
2 Timothy 1:7

Luck

I've never had "good fortune"
Deliver from distress.
But I have known One who's near
To save me and to bless!

I've never seen "a bit of luck,"
Or met a "lucky" man.
But I have known acts of love
From His almighty hand!

I've never known a fluke or chance,
Or random odds to care.
But I have known One who gives,
Before I ask in prayer!

I've never trusted rabbits' feet,
A knock on wood or charms.
But I have rested, oh so oft,
In everlasting arms!

"The Lord is my shepherd; I shall not want."
Psalm 23:1

This Man Receiveth Sinners

"This Man receiveth sinners!"
Oh! Praise forever be!
That means, our Lord of Glory,
He cares for such as we!

Tax collectors! Harlots!
The low from sea to sea!
He proves He is the sinner's friend!
Again! All praises be!

A Lord who loves the down and out;
Each crippled soul He sees!
Our God hath sent His Holy One
For sinners just like me!

No soul's despised, not low nor high,
Who makes the sinner's plea!
Whoever comes repenting true,
He says, "Come unto Me!"

No one's cast off! No one forgot!
He hath remembered thee!
And calls the wretched, you and I,
To come and to be free!

"And the Pharisees and scribes murmured, saying,
This man receiveth Sinners …"
Luke 15:2

The Fellowship of Blood

By blood we are related in communion:
By blood to every Christian we are kin!
One body and one blood we are in union;
Not in our veins, but by the blood of Him!

There is one bride and only one blessed Bridegroom.
One table laid for all among the stars!
And mired souls shall sup within that Kingdom;
All served by Him, whose blessed kin we are!

Oh! May that holy fellowship in Heaven,
Be ours as well to cherish here today!
A bonding now of those who love the Master:
A fellowship of hearts where He doth stay!

"There is one body, and one Spirit, even as ye are called
in one hope of your calling;"
Ephesians 4:4

Do You Know?

"Know ye what I have done to you?"
Asked Christ, who washed their feet.
And He could well ask this of us,
Before His mercy seat!

He's written us into His book,
And come into our souls!
And when our names are called above,
His own He'll surely know!

"Know ye what I have done to you?"
In Heaven ye are kin!
My spirit dwells within your heart:
New life will now begin!

A place I have prepared for you,
That ye may dwell with Me!
A thousand years is but a taste
Of sweet eternity!

"Know ye what I have done to you?"
Now we are brothers true!
You are beloved of My heart
And of My Father's too!

"… know ye what I have done to you?"
John 13:12

A Song of Kindness

Oh, cause me Lord
To sing Thy kindness,
Early in the day.
And put my trust,
In Thee O Lord,
To live a life of praise!

Oh, let me sing
Thy tender care,
With rising of the Sun!
And let me sing
Thy praises yet,
When dark of night has come!

Yea, let me know
Thy mercies Lord,
That see me through my days!
And let me sing
Aloud to Thee,
Who keeps me in His ways!

Oh, grant my song
Be clear and true!
To tell all men, my Lord of You!
My source of love! And all my life!
Who keeps me close,
Both day and night!

"It is a good thing to give thanks unto the Lord, and to sing praises unto thy name, O most High: To shew forth thy loving-kindness in the morning, and thy faithfulness every night."
Psalm 92:1, 2

That Which Saves

Faith is that which saves a soul,
For nothing else will do!
It is the one and only thing,
Can make your life anew!

Faith! A bit as small as seed,
Our own Good Master said,
Can grow just as a mighty tree;
And even raise the dead!

By faith our Master bore the Cross.
His faith saved you and me!
He knew just who His Father was,
And knew what He must be!

He did it all by saving faith!
And gave the same to me!
True faith is such a wondrous thing!
When it is born in Thee!

They say, sight is believing!
And by true faith I see,
His Father's love, and His as well
Who gave Himself for me!

"But without faith it is impossible to please him …"
Hebrews 11:6

His Father's Eyes

He saw them through His Father's eyes,
And not the eyes of flesh.
His mind looked past the lust and sins
In which they were enmeshed.

He saw the breath of God within
And knew He could atone,
For all their wayward sinfulness
And bring the grateful home.

He saw the first held innocence
Of every newborn child;
Beheld the ravages of sin
On beings created mild.

And strove to save
The souls He'd made,
Though fallen now
And vile.

And still He sees through Heaven's eyes,
The likes of you and me;
Beholds us not as now we are,
But what our souls will be;

When once true faith in Him awakes
And eyes at last can see;
A vision of redemption come
And glory that will be!

"And yet if I judge, my judgment is true: for I am not alone,
but I and the Father that sent me."
John 8:16

Father of Lights

Oh! Father of lights, and joy of my life!
Rich gifts through the years, sent to me
Came down from above, Thou Father of love;
Each perfect, as perfect could be!

No shadow of turning, no change of Thy will,
That I should belong unto Thee!
I was soiled by sin, but my love Thou did win,
By the strength of Thy caring for me!

By the blood of Thy Son and the Word of Thy truth,
Thy goodness hath bound me to Thee.
Though poor in this world, I am rich in Thy faith:
A treasure Thou gavest to me!

While I searched in the darkness, Thy love found me out!
Oh! Thy care is as vast as the sea!
By chains of affection, Thou hast made me Thine own!
In Thy bondage at last I am free!

"Every good gift and every perfect gift is from above, and cometh down
from the Father of lights ..."
James 1:17

O Thou the Word of Power

Dear Jesus, save me from myself:
O Thou the Word of power!
Oh, let me walk within Thy will,
From now, this very hour!

I've flung the door upon my soul
And seek to Thee my tower!
Oh! Keep me from my own dark bent;
And him who would devour!

No other hope have I at all:
My saving grace Thou art!
Oh! Take and keep me as Thine own:
And live within my heart!

"Thine O Lord, is the greatness and the power ..."
1 Chronicles 29:11

Twilight Prayer

From the coming of the morning Sun,
To the parting of the same,
The praises of our Mighty One,
Shall ever tell Thy fame.

O Master, Keeper of our hearts;
The Maker of our day,
In Thee we rest, when comes the night,
And breath doth flee away!

We greet Thee in the dawning light,
Fresh come from out the womb!
And Thou art still our dearest friend,
Within the twilight's gloom.

Yours is the Earth, and Yours the stars:
For both were made by Thee!
How precious then, Thy sweet regard
For one as small as me!

I shall not fear the fading light.
I have Thee faithful friend;
In whom there is no dark at all;
And we shall meet again!

"From the rising of the sun unto the going down of the same the Lord's name is to be praised."
Psalm 113:3

All My Days

You who've loved me
All my days,
The Mighty One of all my praise;
I bless Thee!

You whose love has gone before,
Preparing me a way;
The Deity who won my heart
And fed me all my days!

I know not why You've loved me so!
Or why You've never let me go!
But I would praise the friend You be,
And bless you so, for loving me!

Now, please receive this feeble praise,
I send up through the blood!
This man You've called unto Yourself,
And raised up from the mud!

Yea, Father I would offer praise,
Sent through Your worthy Son!
And give You heartfelt thankfulness
For all that You have done!

Oh, let me ever walk with Thee,
My life give ever praise!
And let me be Thy grateful friend,
And bless Thee all my days!

"… the God which fed me all my life long unto this day …"
Genesis 48:15

Your Arms

Underneath me are Your arms.
I feel them about!
You've held me close throughout my years!
Thy love hath found me out!

Oh! Everlasting are Your arms!
And since I know Your care,
Though I grow old and gray in years,
My heart knows no despair!

Throughout my life You've held me close;
And fed me by Your hand!
Despite myself, my life's been blessed.
And by Your grace, I stand!

Almighty Lord, You've always been
My dear and closest Friend!
Oh! Keep me ever close to Thee,
Until You come again!

"The eternal God is thy refuge, and underneath
are the everlasting arms …"
Deuteronomy 33:27

My Lord He Hath Forgiven

My Lord, He hath forgiven me,
    The creature that I am!
Wherever could I hope to find,
    The like of Him again?

My sins cast deep within the sea;
Because, He hath forgiven me!
He knows all secrets of my soul;
Knows more than any other knows!

Yet, walks with me At peace we be!
And from myself, He's set me free.
This truth I'll sing while breath there be.
My Lord, He hath forgiven me!

The heathen fears His karma,
    The superstitious, signs.
And those beneath a crushing guilt,
    Can lose their lives or minds!

I do not balance yin and yang,
    Nor of my life keep score!
Nor hope, somehow, the good I've done,
    Outweighs my sins and more!

No longer seeking tortured climbs.
There is a peace come to my mind.
When guilt and stain He bears away;
The soul at last, can walk in day.

Temptations, now, they lose their power,
When e'er I seek my mighty Tower!
The strength of life, that makes me free?
My lord He hath forgiven me!

"Come now, and let us reason together, saith the Lord: though your sins be as scarlet, they shall be as white as snow …"
Isaiah 1:18

How It Was

I found you in your afterbirth, and chilled near to the bone:
Cast out, unloved, unwanted, with the trash and all alone!

There was odor, there was garbage, there was wailing, you were cold!
So young and so abandoned (perhaps an hour old!)

None else did heed your crying; it was I who found you thus:
And My heart could not resist you! With no parent you could trust!

I cradled you, and fed you, and I washed you gently clean,
And dressed in garments new and soft (you were such a helpless being!)

To you I was a mother, I was Father, and your Friend.
That was how I saved you from the dark. That was how it all began!

Oh, I've given blood to save you! And have called you for My own!
Will you simply let Me love you? Will you let Me take you home?

"When my father and my mother forsake me,
then the Lord will take me up."
Psalm 27:10

"… thou wast cast out in the open field, to the lothing of thy person,
in the day that thou wast born. And when I passed by thee,
and saw thee polluted in thine own blood, I said unto thee
when thou was in thy blood, Live …"
Ezekiel 16:5, 6

The Angel Maker

More than all the flock of Heaven,
Singing choirs shining bright;
Is the Maker of the angels,
Lord of hosts and Lord of might!

More than all the dazzling Seraph,
White as dawn in bright array,
Is the Maker of the angels,
Lord of light and Lord of day!

More than all with wings, who praise Him,
Is Jehovah on His throne!
Holy Maker of the angels,
Lord of all, we are His own!

"And of the angels he saith, Who maketh his angels spirits,
and his ministers a flame of fire."
Hebrews 1:7

Speaking in the Sky

"Good morning Father! Here am I!"
Just now, at break of day,
I wake and talk, with Him unseen.
I guess you'd say, I pray.

His answer? Fire in the sky!
Strange lovely shades of blue,
With burning clouds in shining pink,
And all the woods renewed!

Tall trees of black, no beauty lack!
Sun fire just behind.
Oh, what a way to start the day!
With colors rich and fine.

The Master writes in holy words,
Within His ancient Book.
But also speaks within the sky,
If you will only look!

The glory of the morning,
The peace of sunset time,
And mired stars within the night,
Tell me His love is mine!

The changing light of day and night,
They so declare to me,
That there's a loving Lord above.
If you have eyes to see!

"The heavens declare the glory of God; and the firmament sheweth his handywork. Day unto day uttereth speech, and night unto night sheweth knowledge: There is no speech nor language, where their voice is not heard."
Psalm 19:1–3

There's Hope for All

Born in the dark of hate-filled lands,
Where nightmares live in day,
Our God, He knows where we began,
And why the darkness stayed!

He knows of failed parents;
And fruit of hateful days.
Betrayed by those who ought to love,
Sent early to the grave.

Drugs and drink, a home that reeks
And violence unrestrained;
All this He does consider,
When He looks upon our shame!

Like flowers blooming in the mire,
There's some above it rise!
Their arms upraised, like hopeful plants
While pleading to the skies!

Wounded minds, and wounded souls,
And broken hearts that cry:
He knows it all! More grace poured out,
That hope, it may not die!

The things unknown to our lives,
His laws do not require!
Yet, by the mercy of His love,
He draws His own up higher!

He knows the sorrows of the heart;
The sins that cling and bind!
For He has been the soul's escape,
Throughout the years of time!

A God of wondrous miracles:
Who knows our heart's desire!
And lifts the souls that cling to Him,
To kindle holy fire!

"Save us, O Lord our God, and gather us from among the heathen …"
Psalm 106:47

Witness

We cannot save another man,
Or break his hardened heart.
That is the work of God alone.
That is His Sovereign part!

The most that you or I can do,
Is let His work be seen.
And tell what great things, He hath done,
Like men of Gadarene.

This is the task that He hath set,
For such as you and me.
And this the only way for us
To set another free.

The filthy chains that bound our lives:
Our wounds and ugly sores,
He hath removed, and healed our minds:
Our sanity restored!

And like those men among the tombs,
Back in the days of yore,
We have but gratitude to give,
And praise forever more!

Now, as the man born blind from birth,
Bear simple witness we.
"All that I know, is I was blind.
And now, praise Him! I see!"

"… Jesus … saith unto him, Go home to thy friends, and tell them how great things the Lord hath done for thee …"
Mark 5:19

Piercing of the Heart

All we, have pierced, The holy heart of Father!
For we have surely slain His dear Son!
The One who dwelt beside Him all the ages;
Before the shining stars, or time begun!

The very spear that pierced Our own Messiah;
We drove it through the great I Am as well!
And laid upon our Ancient One in Heaven,
More grievous pain then any words can tell!

Oh, Holy One! You sent Your only treasure;
And we've despised by sin, Your precious gift!
Surely, only Blood of Christ May cleanse us!
And only His dear wounded hands can lift!

"… and they shall look upon me whom they have pierced, and they shall mourn for him, as one mourneth for his only son …"
Zechariah 12:10

There Is a God

There is a God, who has a heart.
No idol He, of stone!
His mercy higher than the stars;
And He is God alone!

There is a God of tenderness,
With healing for the soul!
There is a God who loves the Earth:
A God that we may know!

His thoughts to us are thoughts of peace.
And He can bring our souls release!
From chains of sin and dark of night,
And bring us born anew to light!

There is a God who gave His Son,
To save the willing, every one!
A God beyond all hope or thought,
And yet the God we've always sought!

"For I know the thoughts that I think toward you, saith the Lord,
thoughts of peace, and not of evil …"
Jeremiah 29:11

He Careth Much for You

The misery born of humankind,
And all the grief we sow,
It grieves the heart we call Divine;
The God that all may know.

All human grief, and pain of soul,
Bewildered and afraid;
And all the hurt of human flesh,
That's carried to our grave:

He feels and He knows it well,
His breath it lives in we.
And He the pangs of woe has felt,
For every soul that be!

Our mourning and our sorrow,
Weigh heavy on His heart;
And healing for the soul in grief,
His nature would impart.

Oh come unto the One who cares,
And find a healing true!
There is a God who has a heart,
That careth much for you!

"… his soul was grieved for the misery of Israel."
Judges 10:16

Putting Away

I'm loathe to put away My love!
I hate the thing entire!
It wounds to see My gift of life
Thrown out into the fire!

I hate the hollowness it brings,
To lose those I desire:
The bleakness come unto the mind,
When love at last must tire!

To walk away from caring;
Consigning to the flames,
The very souls that had My love;
Left dying in their shame!

How can I give you up to sin?
How let you go your way?
It never has been in My heart
To simply turn away!

Ah! Even now, My heart cries out,
"Oh, turn to me and stay!"
I am thy God! And I declare,
I hate love put away!

"For the Lord, the God of Israel, saith that he hateth putting away …"
Malachi 2:16

"For the Lord shall rise up … that he may do his work, his strange work; and bring to pass his act, his strange act."
Isaiah 28:21

Father of the King

Now surly, you know our precious Savior!
Whose vesture declares Him "King of Kings."
Who offered Himself for our redemption!
Forever may His holy praises ring!

But have you met the Ancient One of Heaven?
Whose praises, both Son, and angels sing.
The Great One who sent His own to save us!
Oh, have you met the Father of the King?

To know Him and His Son is life eternal!
The Scriptures declare this unto thee;
The Ancient who sit enthroned in Heaven,
And He with wounded hands who died for thee.

"Yahweh," they call Him, or "Jehovah"!
"The Ancient of Days," "The Great I Am"!
Of whom the Master said that, "He so loves you,
He sent His only Son! To be your friend!"

"My Abba! My Deity! My Sovereign!
His endless praise and holiness I sing!
To know Me, is to know the One who sent Me!
Oh, have you met the Father of the King?"

"And this is life eternal, that they might know thee the only true God,
and Jesus Christ, whom thou hast sent."
John 17:3

The Stars Would Weep

I know Your morning stars would weep
And fill the sky with tears,
If I should wander from Your love;
The very thing I fear!

I'd rather seek an open grave,
Then live apart from Thee!
O Thou who art my heart, my life,
Draw closer still to me!

I know I cannot stand alone
Your strength upholds my soul!
You are the secret of my heart:
The only God I know!

Your morning stars rejoice to sing
Of souls who live to serve their King!
Oh! Take my heart, and safely keep!
I would not have Your stars to weep!

"… the morning stars sang together, and all the sons
of God shouted for joy …"
Job 38:7

I AM

Throughout the Earth, His voice proclaims,
To every maid and man,
"Lift up your hearts and look on high,
And know the truth! I AM!"

Mid rock or sand, or fields of green,
His name's proclaimed as when;
Majestic voice of Deity,
First spoke it unto men!

The mighty roar of oceans vast,
The still of forest way;
Proclaim as clear, to ears that hear,
That holy name today!

His myriad stars in midnight skies,
Speak out to questing souls;
The precious truth of One on high,
That every heart may know!

All hope there be, herein is found;
His Son has died for man!
And pleads our case before the throne
Of He, the great I AM!

"And God said unto Moses, I Am That I Am: And he said, Thus shalt thou say unto the children of Israel, I Am has sent me unto you."
Exodus 3:14

"For there is one God, and one mediator between God and men, The man Christ Jesus; who gave himself a ransom for all …"
1 Timothy 2:5, 6

"Wherefore he is able also to save them to the uttermost that come unto God by him, seeing he ever liveth to make intercession for them."
Hebrews 7:25

Daybreak

A day of resurrection comes, when every faithful heart,
Shall see again our loved and lost, rise like a work of art!
To shine and sing, to laugh and cry,
To look with wonder to the sky.
And never more to part!

The night shall fade, the trumpet sound,
The morning come, and there be found;
The dear of heart we laid to rest.
Our kindred, friends, and all the best:
Once given to the ground!

> An end of sorrows and of sighs,
> Restoring love's old precious ties!
> When curse and death He disannul,
> Our Christ shall gather pole to pole,
> All faithful hearts and wise!

"… The hour is coming, and now is, when the dead shall hear the voice of the Son of God: and they that hear shall live. For as the Father hath life in himself; so hath he given to the Son to have life in himself:"
John 5:25, 26

Waiting for the Morning

Waiting for the morning.
Waiting for the light!
Waiting for the Son to come,
And take away the night!

Waiting for the angels;
Holiness to sing!
Waiting till a shining choir
Makes the heavens ring!

Waiting for the morning,
When trumpets fill the sky!
Waiting for our King to come,
Back for you and I!

Waiting to be born aloft,
Upon glad angel wing!
Oh! How our hearts will sing aloud,
When we shall see our King!

"For the Lord himself shall descend from heaven with a shout, with the voice of the archangel, and with the trump of God: and the dead in Christ shall rise first: then we which are alive and remain shall be caught up together with them in the clouds, to meet the Lord in the air: and so shall we ever be with the Lord."
1 Thessalonians 4:16, 17

All My Springs

Thou art my true King,
And all of my springs.
Yea! All of my days
Are in Thee.
For in Thee do I move;
And have all my being:
Yea! Only in Thou
Could I be.

Thou fashioned this dust.
Thy breath Thou hast lent.
The days I have lived,
Were from Thee.
Though skeptics may laugh,
And say there's no God;
They might as well
Say there's no me!

This world Thou hast made.
All thing are of Thee.
The life of all living, Thou art.
This wisdom, I know,
Thou has taught to my mind.
And I know Thou
Art here in my heart!

"… all my springs are in thee …"
Psalms 87:7

"For in him we live, and move, and have our being …"
Acts 17:28

Into the Water for Me

When my life was near taken from me,
Swept away on sin's raging sea;
Before I had been,
You were my loyal friend,
Coming into the water for me!

The billows were mountains above me,
Drowning out the pure light of day!
But Jesus came in
To my nature of sin,
And sought me
Before I could pray!

O Lord who ventured to save me,
And suffered not Satan to win;
The banner You raise,
Calls now for such praise,
That my tongue
Can scarcely begin!

You threw out no lifeline to save me,
Nor advice called out from the shore.
You got your feet wet,
And so they are yet,
Small wonder,
We sing and adore!

"But the ship was now in the midst of the sea, tossed with waves: for the wind was contrary. And in the fourth watch of the night Jesus went unto them, walking on the sea."
Matthew 14:24, 25

The City Whose Maker is God

As Abram, we look for a city,
Whose builder and maker is God!
A city that's spoke of in Scripture:
A passion that marks us as odd!

For this quest, it draws us up higher:
A vision possessing the soul!
And we know who's the Stairway provided,
He's the One way to Heaven! We know!

We look for a land rich in splendor;
And the city of which we've been told:
A gathering of mansions awaiting!
Where the streets are all paved in pure gold!

Here, the Author of all understanding,
Rules a Kingdom of wonders and might!
In whose presence and call, there's no darkness at all,
But only the glory of light!

"For he [Abraham] looked for a city which hath foundations,
whose builder and maker is God."
Hebrews 11:10

A Name for Deity

The only real Deity,
Came down to speak to man.
And said to Moses,
"For My name, just tell them that I Am!"

"Desire of each yearning heart,
Beyond all gods of stone!
I am the God who dwells in you:
And I Am God alone!"

"I Am the Father of the stars;
All beings that dwell on high:
The Giver of all life and breath:
Who knows His children's cry!"

"As for this Earth, whereon you stand;
And everything there in,
I spoke the same, that it might be,
Back when it did begin!"

"I gave a woman unto man,
And gave a man to she!
And every soul that's ever lived;
That soul belongs to Me!"

"And if they ask, 'Whence came your God,
Before all else began?'
The answer you already know!
It's simply this, I AM."

"And God said unto Moses, I Am That I Am: And he said, thus shalt thou say unto the children of Israel, I AM hath sent me unto you."
Exodus 3:14

The Easy Yoke

"Oh, come unto Me
And find your true rest.
I know you are weary;
Your soul so distressed!"

"Your sins are too heavy.
Their weight bears you down!
They'll crush you and press
Your poor heart to the ground!"

"This burden you bear
Is too much laid on thee!
Now come let Me lift it
And set your soul free!"

"My yoke it is easy.
My burden tis light!
Abandon the darkness.
Come out of the night!"

The burden of guilt,
For these of your sins,
Your Father has taken
And laid them on Him!"

"Come unto me, all ye that labour and are heavy laden, and I will give you rest. Take my yoke upon you, and learn of me; for I am meek and lowly in heart: and ye shall find rest unto your souls. For my yoke is easy, and my burden is light."

Matthew 11:28–30

Your Hands

Tonight I'll sleep throughout the storm,
And know Your hands are neigh,
And so, I'll fear no thunder's roar,
Nor lightning in the sky!

Tonight I'll rest in hands of love
And know such wondrous power,
That violence of the mighty storm,
Will seem as lightest shower!

And when the terrible storm of death,
Shall come, faith to devour:
I'll hold those same warm hands of Yours
To keep me in that hour!

The storms of life are grim indeed!
Above they truly tower!
But none can take us from Your hands,
Which hold with loving power!

"… Father, into thy hands I commend my spirit …"
Luke 23:46

My Rest

In Him I find the rest that all men long for:
A rest no other ever could bestow.
He giveth rest for every weary body,
Each fevered mind, and every longing soul.

In Him I find my true and living Sabbath.
A resting from my works, His blood did sow.
Behavior and my deeds, they are not coinage!
My trust is in the Savior that I know.

What He has done on Earth, it has no equal!
It's this I trust today, as at the start.
In Him is all my hope and all my courage,
His strength to keep me ever in His heart.

"… my flesh also shall rest in hope."
Psalm 16:9

Thy Son Our Prayer

O Love above, unfailing,
My prayer I send to Thee!
Look down my Lord in mercy,
Unworthy though I be!

I claim the name of Jesus,
Who shed His blood for me!
Oh! Cover with His righteousness,
This frail thing You see!

Though dust I am, Almighty One,
Yet, pray I this to Thee!
Oh! Cover in His virtue's robe,
This sinner that I be!

Unworthy as a publican,
Yet, know Thy heart doth care!
Accepting we who come to Thee,
And make Thy Son our prayer!

O grant to me Thy prodigal,
A Father's love for me!
Christ came to save the poor in heart:
Ah! Father! This I be!

"… he hath made us accepted in the beloved."
Ephesians 1:6

These Three Remain

These three remain.
These three abide;
In they whom Christ
Hath made alive!

Faith to move the mountains,
That stand before the heart.
Hope in all He hath declared,
While ye were yet apart.

Agape, this His love in thee;
The greatest blessing that there be!
Of these three shining treasures then,
Make most of all, His love thy friend!

For love it doth establish hope,
And causeth faith to be!
Yea! All salvation's power is found,
In His great love for thee!

Have faith in Him who giveth all.
Let hope be strong and free!
But most of all, let love abide:
The greatest of the three!

"And now abideth faith, hope, love, these three;
But the greatest of these *is* love."
1 Corinthians 13:13 (NKJV)

A Rest of the Heart

A rest of the heart,
A rest of the soul,
Oh, cause us O Lord,
Of Thy true rest to know.

Thou keepest of them,
Your word says of Thee,
In Thy perfect peace,
Whose minds are with Thee.

No panic by day,
No terror by night,
Who walk not in darkness;
But in Thy great light.

Thy burden's a feather,
When resteth the heart.
Thy yoke makes it easy,
For all who will hark.

United with Him,
No soul is alone,
For we walk with the Master;
Whose blood hath atoned.

Praise be to the Highest,
Who hath blotted our stains!
Praise be to the Master,
Our rest that remains

"Let us labour therefore to enter into that rest ..."
Hebrews 4:11

Tears

The Word does not declare, "No tears in Heaven!"
For there are tears of joy, as well as pain!
Nor does it say, "There will be no depth of feeling!"
(Just because our hearts are cleansed of guilt and shame.)

It only says, There's One who'll wipe the tear drops
That blight the soul and steal away our joy!
And tears that fall for love ones that are missing:
Who've left within the heart a place that's void.

It does not say "They'll be no glad reunions!"
(That blind the eyes and overwhelm with tears.)
It only says, there's One who knows our feelings,
(And takes our grief and pain, when He draws near.)

All weeping born of pain will surely vanish:
Within the sweet, "Well done!" that greets the ear.
But there are grateful tears of holy gladness,
That ever will be shed in love sincere!

Our very depth of heart will only deepen;
And every trace of stone will disappear!
And smiling tears may come with golden mornings,
And blessed songs our Holy One will hear!

"And God shall wipe away all tears from their eyes; and there shall be no more death, neither sorrow, nor crying, neither shall there be any more pain: for the former things are passed away."
Revelation 21:4

The Living God

All humans need the living God,
Not plaster, wood, or stone.
A God who feeds the hungry heart
And seeks out those alone.

A God who knows the ones He's made:
A God who understands and saves.
A God who seeks the broken soul,
To heal, mend, and make it whole.

We need a God who loves the young:
A tender God for tender ones.
A God who seeks the sick and old:
A God who their afflictions knows.

A God who calls us to His heart,
And hunts for those who live apart.
We need the God who comes within;
Who dwells with us and we with Him.
A God to turn our souls above;
A God whose very name is love!

"… my soul thirsteth for God, for the living God:"
Psalm 42:2

A Grace That's Called Amazing

Your grace is called "Amazing."
The comfort of our hearts!
And with it You did keep our souls,
When we walked far apart!

There's grace for those who wander,
As those who know You well!
And it's been ours from out the womb,
More grace than we can tell!

Your grace, it keeps our frail lives,
From one who'd tear asunder!
And comes to us in tender love,
Far more than in the thunder!

Your grace beholds our tears that fall:
A grace that giveth breath to all!
Your grace is found where e'er we go;
And meets the deepest needs we know!

It's faithfulness it turns our minds
And maketh all things new!
This thing we call "amazing grace";
Pure kindness come from You!

"And of his fullness have all we received, and grace for grace."
John 1:16

Lover of My Soul

Today I found the heart I sought
The Lover of my soul;
And sweeter He, and more to me,
Than any that I know!

Today I found someone to love,
Who, always did love me!
And never have I known joy,
As this He giveth free!

He found me in a lonely place;
Yet, with a teeming crowd.
He found me wandering with the lost,
And called my name aloud!

And now I walk within His warmth,
His hand in all I see!
Who knows each corner of my soul
And sins that now I flee!

He's made my world a grand new place:
No longer steeped in night!
But lit with purpose of His will,
And bathed in holy light!

I know He plans another world,
Where all His own shall be.
But now, I rest within these arms
That hold and cherish me!

"… I found him whom my soul loveth …"
Song of Solomon 3:4

The Rock of Israel

Thou art the Rock of Israel.
And Oh! My Rock as well!
In vain upon my Mighty Lord,
Do rage the storms of Hell!

Those winds no longer bend my will.
I'm building on my Rock.
And clinging to that mighty stone,
Upon the sand I'm not!

Almighty One! Thou art my Rock!
Foundation firm for man.
Thou art the secret of my soul,
And by Thy grace I stand!

My Rock of ages towers
Above the fears of men!
Come to the Rock and fear ye not.
He is thy mighty Friend!

"… lead me to the rock that is higher than I. For thou hast been a shelter for me, and a strong tower from the enemy."
Psalm 61:2, 3

Behold the Man

Behold,
A Man who once was Sacred Spirit.
Behold!
A Man who caused the stars to be.
Behold!
A Man who sits enthroned in Heaven.
Behold,
The Man who gave Himself for me!
Behold,
A Man who walked with lowly sinners.
Behold!
A Man who set those sinners free!
Behold!
The angels bowing low before Him.
Behold!
The Man who bore the Cross for thee!
Behold,
The Man in who we are accepted.
Behold!
Our King, forevermore to be!
Behold!
The hope of Abraham and Moses.
Behold!
The Son of God! For this is He!

"… And Pilate saith unto them, behold the man!"
John 19:5

The Way Home

I'll reach the home prepared for me,
But, by the One who built it!
A place He hath prepared for us,
And by His blood He'll fill it!

A list of deeds, all done in Christ,
Cannot my passage buy!
To gates above, or Earth remade;
No matter how I'd try!

My sweat, my tears, a martyr's blood!
Though well, could not avail.
I cling but to His Mighty Cross,
And blood that cannot fail!

He came, He lived, He bled, and died:
Thus, for my sins atoned!
And He it is, by blood alone,
Will finally bear me home!

"… the church of God, which he hath purchased with his own blood."
Acts 20:28

We invite you to view the complete
selection of titles we publish at:
www.TEACHServices.com

We encourage you to write us
with your thoughts about this,
or any other book we publish at:
info@TEACHServices.com

TEACH Services' titles may be purchased in
bulk quantities for educational, fund-raising,
business, or promotional use.
bulksales@TEACHServices.com

Finally, if you are interested in seeing
your own book in print, please contact us at:
publishing@TEACHServices.com
We are happy to review your manuscript at no charge.

www.ingramcontent.com/pod-product-compliance
Lightning Source LLC
Chambersburg PA
CBHW071848230426
43671CB00012B/2104